# Last Days

## of a House

*Manuel Adrian Lopez*

**Last Days of a House**
**Copyright © 2021 Manuel Adrian Lopez**
**ISBN: 978-1-970153-35-4**

Cover Art - Adonis Muiño Romero
Un Dia Sin Redes/ A Day Without Internet
Mixed Media on Linen, 16 x 26

*Maison*

La Maison Publishing
Vero Beach, Florida
The Hibiscus City
lamaisonpublishing@gmail.com

*Last Days of a House* is a composition of the modern challenge of rootlessness and despair. The poetic subject, the islander, explores a new home in the supposed welcoming Upper Manhattan, a place that all too often seems meaningless. This collection reflects a double consciousness, that is perceiving and judging a city full of unnamed wounded men of multicultural backgrounds that unleash desire and dejection where their inhabitants have lost its way home.

Ivonne Gordon
Ecuadorian Poet - Author of *Water House*

"Whether surveying the contours of New York cityscapes—where one longs for a "a dose of warmth/ directions to Staten Island / or a welcome pat"—or excavating the crumbling interior of a marriage "as fragile as sugar glass," the poems in *Last Days of a House* never fail to illuminate the bonds that both bind in union and dissolve in entropy. López's speaker, having had "their perfect idyll" shattered, has the courage to endure at "the crossroads of their fears," waiting for someone to come along and "pick up the pieces of this dilapidated / house" that they've become."

Jonathan Simkins
Writer and Translator

"In this *poemario*, physical geography and virtual yearning come together under the umbrella of verses that are wise without being cynical. Poems that pierce, slice, and dissect. Manuel's gaze becomes obsessed with characters that swarm the lyrical space, exposing them to a fiery, scrutinizing view that, like the magnifying glass that concentrates de ray of light on the paper, burns everything around. I have read this collection under the impression that art is a matter of elevation and a double-edged sword. This book is a bird whose eyes have just been gouged out, but it is also the winged hope that comes through a broken mirror."

Rey Andújar
Worker. Fighter.

*Security is a false God. Begin to make sacrifices to it, and you are lost.*
Paul Bowles

# Table of Contents

## The New York of his dreams

did not include

*bodegas* on every corner.

Nor being a witness

to drug selling.

Transactions made

while policemen

checked out Latina's prominent assets.

The soundtrack of the New York in his

dreams

did not include

the sound of *bachata*.

He longed for Sinatra

and *Strangers in the Night*.


He screamed on Ellwood Street.

On Broadway.

Right off Dyckman and Nagel.

He ached.

**February has passed and forgotten**

the snow covered the thrash

and the starved roaches.

Only the three-legged table

made its presence known.

It was evenly quiet

a desert heading to the altar.

The supposed ideal pad

caught in between hills

and dreams

never dreamt.

They both repeated over and over

to themselves

and others waiting for a report

on their latest undertaking:

It's across from Fort Tryon Park

across from the Cloisters

and its bloody unicorn tapestries.

If they only knew then

the silence was about to be broken

the house was about to crumble

their perfect idyll shattered.

**Boxes opened**

remnants of treasures

jigsaw puzzle-like

ripping thru the newspaper

bearing repetitive news of the island.


Our blood-stained hands holding

the outline of days past.

A vintage Italian vase

with sculpted fuchsia flowers

fell right into the makeshift trashcan.

The one-of-a-kind robotic sculpture

decapitated itself while starring

at the nosy neighbor

exposing her middle-aged breasts

on the fire escape.

## Two closets apart for the married couple

a wall intersects them
the stench of abused dogs
clings to every garment.
Clothing meant for another climate.
Shoes that no longer perform
on sidewalks bruised with black ice.
Two closets apart for the married couple
just like the dynamite-ridden trench
that separates them.

**The cat learned to speak in the city**

from the window leading to the fire escape.

She wandered about

befriending pigeons

that fluttered their wings in salute.

She walked about listening.

The cat learned to resist in the city

hiding under the covers

not understanding his screams.

## They were not expecting a red-carpet affair

they didn't want to borrow twenty bucks
they had enough food in the refrigerator
to last them a good three months.
They learned new lessons in the city.
Loneliness reached a new dimension.
Friends vanished
afraid that the new arrivals
would stick a needle in their eyes
or steal a silver fork
or a piece from their treasured china
smuggled secretly from the island.

All they longed for was a dose of warmth
directions to Staten Island
or a welcoming pat.

**When does it end?**
he asked repeatedly
while lighting a candle every Monday
to Eleggua.

How does it end?
while snoring in his designated spot
on the bed that croaks.

**Cave-like interior**

brownish crater

embalms the body

watching swallows flying low

over his cracked head.

Clay images.

Hollow.

Bursting

as he walks down Park Avenue.

Inappropriate clothing.

Improper stare.

An unhappy man.

**I am willing to admit I'll fall for any man**

offering a five-minute reward.

Bear hugs

would be the most compelling fantasy.

Instead

I invest my free time in stares.

Strangers flash by

at the speed of the A train.

**Altars in every corner**

candles with saints painted on

carnations galore

cardboard makeshift banners

announcing the dead.

Crying time is designated

in 15-minute intervals.

A reward:

Cheap rum to any passerby

that salutes solemnly.

**Inwood is a Pollock painting**

the divine abode of the dead.

Once silent film's backyard

Houdini's wife's hideout.

Another address for La Divina.

Elise Cowen's last breath.

Poets find their way

into dilapidated buildings.

Irish pubs

red-haired inhabitants… gone.

Islanders bathe in the summer

out by fire hydrants.

Rats have a hard time making it

this far up north.

When it snows

a blanket mummifies the stench

of cannabis.

West of Broadway

one can run into the Orthodox.

Bearded ones

always looking at the sidewalk

never at one's eyes.

**A twenty-six-year-old Dominican**

begs for someone to knock on his

door on Sherman Street

and relieve their needs on him.

Just ring the bell.

Enter

and piss all over his cherubic face.

Ease his longing for punishment

other than his drunken father's beatings

or his uncle's dirty fingernails

as they find their way.

**An army of empty beer bottles**

noticeable sweat drops

semen

decorating the staircase.

The banister shines with the greasy rice

residuals

the once elegant marble

is stained with drops of blood.

The trash bags fly from the fifth floor.


A couple of volunteers

fiercely rummage

through everyone's thrash

collecting enough bottles

to pay for their next fix.


The dead beg for a candle

or a wilted flower to ease their path.

**Screams start about three am**

a serenade of abuse

without a violin

infected lungs that roar

begging for the princess

to let him in.


She succumbs to his music

and later to his fists.


She swallows every pill

down with beer

on a Saturday at noon.

*Tigeres* stare as he passes by

fondling themselves

with wicked smiles.

Long sideburns

gangster-like sunglasses.

Their shoes mimic the Pope´s Prada's.


Tiny cigarettes dangling from their full lips

pants reaching the sidewalk

leaving their action heroes buttocks

exposed.


Unappealing men

at the corner

at the crossroads

at death´s grasp.

**Cherry blossoms in pairs**

skunks holding their paws

red cardinals

French-kissing in the air

while he sits on a bench

on the prowl

for any accomplice

who would be willing to appease

his gloom.

**As you open the living room shades**

a sultry neighbor

does her pissing routine

in a jar

outside your window

while the soundtrack plays:


*Escucha las palabras De Romeo*

*The King stays King, yes sir.*

*Llora*

# The gray-haired bus driver

from Yonkers

speaks four languages

flashes his pearly whites

and he may be the lover

the long-distance

tarot card reader

predicted.

He covers the meter with his hands

this time is on him.

He keeps tabs

thru the rear-view mirror

squints

as he fights traffic

and the Harlem River

witnesses

a game of useless flirting.

**Elmer's glue held the foundation**

questionable from its start.

One lacked endurance

the other was running away

from a man with a nervous tic.


At the crossroads of their fears

they built a life

fragile as one's ego.


The base is caving in

as they have forgotten

that which unites them.

## Cries of hunted men by the Hudson River

chained to the bottom of the filthy waters

entangled with used condoms

and leftover tostones

islander's day by the riverbank.

Horse´s gallops in mid-air

while he strolls by the solitary trail

confined to voices

in need of a conversation.

**A year of silence**

nods at dinner time

in front of the television

muddled-headed with breaking news.


Election season and its jesters

a dying Prince

and the takeover of the island by the white

man

while in their house all crumbles:


No gas

intermittent heating

lack of hot water for a bath

and kidnapped caresses

by a sinister militant.

**Confession time comes sporadically**

when the rope breaks

when the spirits whisper in his ear.

Spying time.

A little boy caught red-handed

he inquires

and forgets that his touch has been absent.

Flashing images

he recalls and asks

¨How come you don´t touch my penis

anymore? ¨

**Demolished images**

playing the happy couple

arms on his shoulder

in photographs taken on sporadic outings

later decorating the Facebook wall.


The eternal chorus

never imagining

the real drought behind their smiles.

## Alone sessions

while the cat stares from the windowsill.

A diabetic craving rice pudding

a sick person in need of touch

a myopic staring at any trouser fly.


Strangers in pursuit:

older men with unruly beards

and velvety kippahs

a ghostly Chinese

a black man in orange shorts.


There is no cure.

## Blue sheets

white
crumpled alike
messy balls of damp cloth

stained with coffee drops
marked his and his.

One turns his back
the other lies facing the ceiling
making silent conversation
with the shadows.
Occasionally feeling
his wilted forest.
Turning on his side
mimicking the other.

Wasted lives.
Decomposed.

**Everything revolves around the bed**

and its dusty nightstand holding court.

Tons of unread books

chipped statue of Saint Lucia

whose eyes no longer see.


Afraid to face what awaits

both question themselves in silence:


Who will commit adultery first?

# Soundtracks vary according to the days

Nina's wailing suffices

to torture the other

over and over

it plays:

"If I should lose you...."

as if to drown his presence

his constant aches.

On the scarce downtime

he listens to Little Jimmy

or Archie Shepp

while he scrounges

for a prescription

to an end.

**Only once did their tongues meet**

swirling inside their mouths

eyes closed

sloppy five minutes

obligated exchange

to appease the other

to keep the roof over his head.

**He promised freshly brewed coffee to San Lazaro**

a shining red apple to Santa Barbara
five rum-filled cakes to la Caridad

and flowers galore for all.

He needs a guidebook
on how to end it amicably.
Coelho quotes.
He begs for a white flag
made with an old raggedy Fruit of the Loom
that has not been stained
since they first met.

## No drugs

unless you count

the eight types of pills

to control my sweetness

to dominate my blood vessels

while my insides are sprouting.


Fields of dry corn

as the skin on my feet.

Blooming venom shrubs

silently condemning our marriage

made in New York City Hall.

**He can't recall exactly when the other said**

"Only a year"

He never confided

the contents running at full speed.

He thought the other could read minds.

He thought the other was invincible.

He honestly thought they were one.

**On that seventh day in July**

the poet asked his dead grandfather

for a dose of joy

materializing

in a young priest with a smile.

A young priest that set out

to discover him

as he turned the pages of his Kindle

consuming poison

a drop per page.

**Free tarot readings on the web**

on the phone from afar

the spirits speak loudly

as he walks down Lexington Avenue

as he stands on the corner of 33rd and 3rd

waiting for his next victim.


He must put an end

to what ails him.

A younger darker man is on the horizon

a happy man

with a knack for wine

with tools to get him out of the hole

he has carved out for himself.


Words flutter around him

putting it in practice is a challenge.

He has discarded the Philippine

the gray-haired bus driver

and the persistent shadow of the poet

that was left behind.


After today's reading

he is counting on the young Honduran

poet

to whisk him off to the Hudson River

shore

read Bukowski's "Pulp"

and listen to Vicentico and Willie's song

while they figure out how to crawl.

## A magician is what he was

a trick up his sleeve

a lie dressed up

in Sunday's best.

Spirits were called upon

and discarded

unless he had the winning card.

Unless the other believed blindly

all that was concocted

a blend of control twirled in

with good old survival.

The game thinned out

like the monogrammed terry cloth robe

barely touched

barely worn

perennial solitude on the hook

behind the bathroom door.

**A burning five-year candle**

smiling back at him

atop a chocolaty cake

on that morning

on that ninth day in August.


The poet could have won an acting award

as he fidgeted with what to feel first.


He blew the candle as expected

for the last time.

Obedience

was ending abruptly.

**There are many things to think about**

eternal lists to draft

the impertinent questions:

Who keeps the cat?

Who takes the copper skillet?

## On the street

on Twitter

at the drugstore counter

across the aisle on the bus

at the Salvadorian restaurant

while he notices

at the one jogging with a dangling dong

co-workers that take notice

strangers in black cloth

praying on opposites pews

a young priest

the aspiring writer with an afro

a Philippine with a bad foot

Taneda Santoka and his haikus

one or two Catalans

and a suicidal poet

on the prowl for a life vest.

Smoked salmon

once a month as a prize.

An occasional escapade

at lunchtime

to the barbecue joint.

Straight-faced

avoiding stares

knowing the deficiency

and accepting

that it might linger

for a much longer time

than expected.

Meanwhile

the voices commanding positions

on the other end.

**He burned all meals**

salty steaks

uncooked brown rice

unsalted pasta

unsavory

disillusioned man

pretending to be a cook

hanging on

as the houses collapses.

# Masturbating is less painful

than touching someone's skin.

Is not considered cheating

is it?

You simply hang up after the last cry

of ecstasy.

If by any chance you run into him again

go straight to business.

Succumb to the demands on the other end

let him take charge this time

feel the slap

as if it were being given.

Create a character

depending on the classified answered.

A soft-spoken young boy

or maybe an older divorced man

with a beer gut.

Advertise your fantasy

let it breathe out into the open

and wait for responses to pour in.

Pretend on cyberspace

to have the perfect life

even though your marriage

is as fragile as sugar glass.

Use your time alone productively

answer as many strangers as possible

play the vixen

or the torturer on cue.

Half an hour before the husband returns

take a warm bath

erase any trace of pleasure.

Clorox your perverted thoughts

until the following Saturday

past nine.

## Seven churches in a day

holy water

on your forehead

the blossoming pimple

a unicorn's horn

on your neck

tension wrapped in a meaty ball.

¨Take your Eleggua along

explain to the boy saint

as you stop in every altar:

What is it that you long for?

What is it that you need cured? ¨

Share the benches with the homeless man

pray to the Infant Jesus of Prague

touch his silky green robe

but do not attempt to steal him.

Pretend to walk the streets feeling an air of
triumph
sit on the bus bench
and listen to the woes
of the Mexican couple.
Occasionally
the soprano at the school of music
interrupts.

Disguise yourself as a free man
as you enter church number five
and a chocolaty younger man
offers to give you a tour.
Take his hand in yours
even if it´s just a brief shake.
Lower your eyes
mimicking the low tide
as he scrutinizes you.

He reeks of molasses
from the Caribbean Sea.
Stand in the doorway
look back
and wave to him
as they do in old Hollywood films.

Walk to the next church
expectant
less beaten by your truth
less watered down
hopeful.

Do your part if you care to survive
call the smiling man
leave your number for a rainy day.
He calls back
married with two children

and not a single plan to change that.

But he can´t seem to stop thinking of you.


Your head is in the sewer.

Drag your feet to the last stop.

The church where the nun lies heartless

is shut.

Ride the A train to 207th street

run up the steps to the Good Shepherd

as fast as you can

the door is securely locked.

There are fewer options at hand

but you must strive to reach the seventh

stop.

On the bus

amid the screaming children

and the sad women in nurse's uniform

you remember one close by.

Crawl into a pew
watch the local color chant.
Collapse.

You have reached the seventh church
in a day's challenge.

You are still alive.

**Find a lawyer to file a claim**

there are no children to fight custody for

unless you count the feline.

No savings accounts

or IRA´s

and all stocks were cashed in

to escape.


The photographs of a wailing Queen of

Latin Soul

and the Cuban paintings

are somewhere displayed in the Bay area

at the office of an American tycoon.


Open your own checking account

install a security question on your laptop

call Con Edison and have the services

switched

destroy a house built on camaraderie
instead of ardor.

**He once received**

a red box —

a velvety heart

with stale cherry-filled milk chocolate.


This year

he rode the early train

Made it downtown alone —

unless you count the extras

on their way to work.


Stood in line inside the building

numbed.


This past Valentine's Day

he celebrated in court

filing for divorce.

**The electric can opener disappeared**

tuna cans had to be pried apart

at the neighbors —

a block away.


Grandfather´s cross has taken flight

packed tightly with the saint´s stones

and the little rooster

that supposedly owned the poet´s head.


A reddish blender was shipped

to a broken home

where he was never well-received.


He is aware of the transactions.

The artist versus the obese liar

sweat a little for a new toy.

There are no secrets.

There are no more tales.

**He is a walking archive**

each punch

 files

 in designated slots:

at the very bottom

a poet that he will never kiss


 Then the alcoholic

clairvoyant

 her breasts exposed

 during a session

 to find him a cure for love


to the ex-husband who fled

with the amulets:

let's give slot number eight

 Obbatala's number

 to remember his indifference.

**Bamboo tree**

long-lasting

unbeatable

enduring

although they think of me

as fragile.


A fragile Queer.


The AIDS-stricken poet

shouts

calling me a crying faggot

for all to hear.


A courageous Queer is what I am.


One would think the enemy

did not belong to his own tribe.

## Detox

no more lethal situations

keep most people at a distance.

Time to be indoors

embracing the Bowles

on your shelves.


No real confessions

during walks by the Hudson.

Pretend.

If Gwyneth Paltrow got an Oscar

so can you.

**No formal education to speak of**

unless one counts the many books read.

He is not a bored manic housewife.

Sexton and him

have tons in common

yet his sexual life is not comparable to hers

and she had the courage to end it all at

forty-five

something he tried at twenty-seven

and failed.

No inheritance from a wealthy parent

unless one counts his mother's checks

hidden inside Mother's Day cards

sent to him from time to time.

No lovers holding juicy positions in

the academic field

or at Paz Poetry Prize
who's superior to others
having only one judge.

No critics favoring his work
in any language.
He is nonexistent for most of his peers
born on the same hellish island.
They've all gambled continuously
wondering
as to when will he stop writing
altogether.

No formal education to speak of
unless you breathe under his breath
unless you walk inside his shoe
with the tiny hole on top
unless you wear his diabetic socks

unless you caress his bad foot

unless you share the loneliness

unless you attend the nightly nightmares

from the first row

unless you hold him long enough

to realize poetry

is the only reason

beside his cat

to pretend.

**Ele told him clearly early on**

Get a hold of a giant strainer

and use it on anyone.

You will be wiser

but extremely lonely.


Ele had all the answers

and cancer did not do her in

as most people thought.


Dark forces did.


I rather jump into the Hudson's chilly

waters

than shelter again

similar forces

under my roof.

### ...And you sit in the dark

Rufus Wainwright sings every single
word you would have said
or written
and cannot.
...and you sit uncomfortably
switching positions in the sofa bed
the one you haven't told the young poet
about
hoping he would share your bed
needing someone else's nightmares
other than your own.
...and you sit with your feet up in the red
chair
the cat runs wildly
thrusting herself against the walls
not eating her favorite food
and licking your t-shirt thirstily.

…and you wonder what is happening all
around you

the silence you have implemented on
others

humidity and its persistence

your aching bones

your feet tingling past midnight

you are running on empty.

… and you stand in front of the mirror

without a clue who this man is

you have never seen him in such disrepair

white hairs are blooming in unexpected
fields

his loneliness is appalling

his arms tired as flags

flags undulating in third-world countries

countries like Upper Manhattan

where destruction is imminent

where men hide out in the paths up above

in the park

solemnly waiting

for any passerby to caress their bulges.

… and you sit touching yourself in places

that have not been touched in years

realizing that you could still sense

the cat sits across from you stoically

and stares knowing all that you don't

… and you fall asleep amid the chaos

asking for a mechanic to knock on your

door

a Japanese poet

an islander of some sort

to pick up the pieces of this dilapidated

house

you've become.

**Manuel Adrián López** was born in Morón, Cuba in 1969. He is a bilingual poet and writer. His work has been published in various literary journals in Spain, United States and Latin America. His published books are: *Yo, el arquero aquel* (Editorial Velámenes, 2011), *Room at the Top* (Eriginal Books, 2013), *Los poetas nunca pecan demasiado* (Editorial Betania, 2013. Awarded Gold Medal by Florida Book Awards in 2013), *El barro se subleva* (Ediciones Baquiana, 2014) and *Temporada para suicidios* (Eriginal Books, 2015), *Muestrario de un vidente* (Proyecto Editorial La Chifurnia, 2016), *Fragmentos de un deceso/El revés en el espejo,* book in conjunction with Ecuadorian poet David Sánchez Santillán for the collection Dos Alas (El Ángel Editor,

2017), *El arte de perder/The Art of Losing* (Eriginal Books, 2017), *El hombre incompleto* (Dos Orillas, 2017), *Los días de Ellwood* (Nueva York Poetry Press, 2018), *Un juego que nadie ve* (Ediciones Deslinde, 2019-2020), and *El abismo en los dedos* (Eriginal Books, 2020).

His poetry has been included in the anthologies: *La luna en verso* (Ediciones El Torno Gráfico, 2013) and *Todo Parecía. Poesía cubana contemporánea de temas Gay y lésbicos* (Ediciones La Mirada, 2015), *Voces de América Latina Volumen II (*Media Isla Ediciones, 2016*), NO RESIGNACIÓN. Poetas del mundo por la no violencia contra la mujer* (Ayuntamiento de Salamanca, 2016) and *Antología Paralelo Cero 2017* (El Ángel Editor).

He has participated in various literary events, such as Miami Book Fair International, XXXV Feria Internacional del Libro del Palacio de Minería in Mexico City, IV Festival Atlántico de Poesía de Canarias al Mundo in Gran Canaria, Spain, V Festival de Poesía de Lima in Perú, Poesía en Paralelo Cero 2017 in Ecuador and Poetry of the Americas, a bilingual poetry reading at the New York Public Library and Festival Internacional de Poesía en Puerto Rico, 2018.

CPSIA information can be obtained
at www.ICGtesting.com
Printed in the USA
BVHW061949070322
630867BV00001B/71

9 781970 153354